VOTE FOR ME!

WRITTEN BY
LOUISE SPILSBURY

ILLUSTRATED BY
MIKE GORDON

WAYLAND

D1354626

Published in paperback in Great Britain in 2019
by Wayland

Text copyright © Hodder and Stoughton 2017
Illustrations copyright © Mike Gordon 2017

Wayland, an imprint of
Hachette Children's Group
Part of Hodder and Stoughton
Carmelite House
50 Victoria Embankment
London EC4Y 0DZ

Wayland Australia
Level 17/207 Kent Street
Sydney, NSW 2000

Managing editor: Victoria Brooker
Creative design: Paul Cherrill

ISBN: 978 1 5263 0213 7

MIX
Paper from
responsible sources
FSC
www.fsc.org   FSC® C104740

Printed in Dubai

An Hachette UK Company
www.hachette.co.uk
www.hachettechildrens.co.uk

CONTENTS

FOLLOW THE LEADER?

If an alien landed on your street and said 'Take me to your leader', like they do in cartoons, what would you do? Would you take them to see your parents, a teacher or the police? In fact, the leaders of a country are the people that run or govern that country. (That's why they are called the government!) What do you know about governments and how they work?

WHY DO WE NEED GOVERNMENTS?

The government of a country is the group of people who make laws and take important decisions about how to run a country. Some people think that politics is confusing and complicated or nothing to do with them, but a government's choices affect almost every part of our lives, every day, even if we are not aware of it. So how do governments work and why do we need governments telling us what to do?

If there were no governments, most people would treat others as they would like to be treated, but some people would take advantage. Imagine what could happen on the roads if there were no speed limits. Or if someone stole something and there were no police or laws against theft. How would you get it back?

← *Did you know that world governments have appointed people to be the first point of contact for aliens trying to communicate with Earth. So, if an alien from a spaceship knocks on your door you can find out who the green Martians should speak to!*

4

GOVERNMENTS IN ACTION

Governments make and enforce rules about what people can and cannot do and make sure that people obey those laws so that people in a community can live together peacefully and safely. For example the roads people drive on, the trucks that collect household rubbish and the schools they attend are, in most areas of the world, maintained or overseen by governments. The government has to defend the country and organise an army to protect it in times of war. It looks after important services like healthcare and education and controls trade and relations with other countries.

So how did governments come about and how do governments work? How do they get into power and how do they use it? How and when did governments begin and become what they are today? Read on to find out …

Governments are the group of people who run a country.

Good To Know

These are some key words to do with governments that it's good to know.

Citizen: a person who legally belongs to a country and has the rights and protection of that country

Government: the people in power, the people given authority over other people

Politics: the actions and policies of a government or getting and keeping power in a government. We also say someone's opinions about what governments should do are their 'politics'.

Society: the people of a country make up the society of that country

State: a nation or territory under one government

HUNTER-GATHERERS

The first modern humans were hunter-gatherers. They were nomadic, moving around from place to place and hunting animals and gathering wild plants for food. Their groups, or societies, were smallish and comprised of several families. Experts believe that these very early societies didn't have rulers or leaders as such, because they found food together and relied equally on each other. There was only just enough food to go around and people had few belongings, so there was less to argue about. There were so few people in the world that experts think that there were no wars over land. People tended to help each other and share what they had, because life was tough and everyone knew that they would need help one day.

Instead of having rulers, it's likely that different people took a leading role at different times if and when different skills were needed. So, one person might have taken the lead temporarily to make choices about where to hunt or to find a cave to spend a cold winter in, if they had some good ideas and so long as the rest of the group agreed. Their decisions would have been based on the best of everyone, not just themselves.

↑ Experts think that most early hunter-gatherer societies would not tolerate anyone trying to lord it over the rest of the group. If one person tried to boss everyone around for too long, the others would make fun of them until they became humble again!

SETTLING DOWN

Over time, people who had been hunters and gatherers gradually discovered how to be farmers. They worked out that they could keep seeds from the plants they collected and grow their own plants and that they could control and breed some of the animals they hunted. When they became farmers, they began to settle in one place, near the fields they tended. Farming transformed the way humans lived. More food meant more mouths could be fed so populations grew and larger communities and villages developed. With larger numbers of people living closer together, there were inevitably more conflicts, possibly made worse by the fact that different communities took water from the same rivers, so they squabbled over these valuable water resources. There were no governments yet, so local priests were probably called on to help settle disagreements.

★ ★ ★ ★ ★ ★ ★ ★ ★ ★ ★ ★ ★ ★ ★ ★ ★ ★

Cradles of civilisation

The first major farming communities in the world were in river valleys in modern-day southern Iraq, Syria, Lebanon, Jordan, Israel and northern Egypt. Land around rivers that flooded every year was fertile and could grow lots of crops, so large populations were concentrated in a comparatively small area. People built irrigation channels, long ditches that carried water to their fields, to be able to grow crops all year round.

★ ★ ★ ★ ★ ★ ★ ★ ★ ★ ★ ★ ★ ★ ★ ★ ★ ★

↑ *In many ancient cultures, priests probably settled disputes and made judgements.*

CITY-STATES

As communities got bigger, they changed. As farmers grew more food, people could do other jobs, such as making tools and constructing buildings, buying their food from the farmers. Gradually, village centres where priests and others had often settled disputes became more powerful. They sorted out more problems and began to manage the building and repair of new dams, ponds and irrigation channels. These village centres gradually became centres of power known as city-states.

These were made up of large, walled cities with a temple and a palace. Leaders, their relatives, priests and other powerful people lived in the city and governed it and the villages around it. As city-states got bigger, tensions arose over land between different centres of power, which sometimes resulted in wars. City-states started to employ armies of soldiers, and equip them with weapons. Farmers and other ordinary people had to contribute money, food or their time to pay for these armies.

After the harvest, farmers in a city-state often had to set to work constructing some of the buildings that made the centre of their city-states, like a capital city today, look impressive and powerful.

Sumerian super powers

In the Sumerian city-states of ancient Mesopotamia, the most powerful people were the ruling class and priests. The middle class was made up of merchants, officials, and craftspeople, while most people were farmers.

While the farmers could and did own and work their own land away from the cities, they also often had to farm government-owned land as well, or work on building the ruler's palaces and other fancy buildings.

OFFICIALS AND LAWS

The governments that ran city-states grew more complex as time went on. Different officials controlled or supervised more and more of their citizens' lives. As well as using people to build their cities, governments often took control of the surplus food that farmers grew, so they could calculate how much there was, store and distribute it. They collected payments from their people to run the state. Officials developed writing in order to keep records and to list the laws that people had to follow in order to keep peace among people living close together and ensure that everyone, regardless of who they were, had some protection from their neighbours and outsiders.

King Hammurabi, who ruled the area now known as Iraq, made the first set of laws in around 2000 BCE. The Code of Hammurabi is carved onto a 2-metre tall rock slab and it sets down harsh penalties for anyone who broke the laws: an eye for an eye and a tooth for a tooth." In other words the punishment fit the crime.

AROUND THE WORLD

Ever since the first city-states, there have been different types of government. Some rulers were priest kings, or kings who claimed to be living gods like the pharaohs. The Minoan culture in ancient Greece gave positions of power to the people who they considered the most talented.

Given that the Minoans were a trading nation this meant the people most skilled at trading came to rule. Over time and as states grew bigger and more complex there have been lots of different kinds of governments, and there still are today. People's ideas about what makes a good government have changed over time, too.

TYPES OF GOVERNMENT

Throughout history, a number of different styles of government developed around the world. The way a government works and how much power and influence it has over citizens' lives varies in different political systems. Some countries have a combination of two or more styles of government and a country with one type of government might change to another!

GOVERNMENTS TODAY

Governments usually have a leader. They are the figurehead of the government and take responsibility for the government's successes and failures. The leader of a government has different names depending on what type of government a country has. Of course, one person cannot be an expert on all the decisions a government has to take, so the leader has a team of politicians who work with him or her to make and change laws.

A government is divided up into departments. Each department is responsible for a different area of life, such as employment, education, arts, sports, the environment, defence etc. Paid civil servants carry out the work of each govermentment department. Each department or sector may work with groups of independent experts who do studies on issues such as protecting the environment and making sure there are enough jobs for everyone. These groups can then advise the government about different courses of action they could take.

There are different styles of government but almost all are made up of departments that deal with different types of decisions, such as education or defence.

ANARCHY!

Sometimes, after a civil war when different groups in the same country fight each other, or when a government has been destroyed and rival groups are fighting to take its place, a country has no government. A situation where there is no government is called anarchy. Anarchy comes from Greek words, which mean 'without rule'. Some people are anarchists, and believe that we don't need rulers telling us what to do. Most anarchists believe that governments are unnecessary and sometimes do bad things. Left alone, they think people would survive by cooperating with each other and following 'natural' laws, for example that we each have the right to live, to be free, and to own our own property. In reality, anarchy has never been successful long-term because it has flaws. For example, if someone stole your bike, how would you get it back if there were no police force to help you?

Other political systems

In this chapter we look at the main political systems but, throughout history, there have been many more besides!

Aristocracy: government based on birth and privilege

Oligarchy: rule by a small group of either related persons or people with a common interest

Despotism: rule by an individual who considers all people his or her slaves

Plutocracy: government ruled by the wealthy

Why do we need someone to tell us what to do? What would life be like without rules and laws? Anarchists believe that without government people would do what is best for society as a whole, but many people believe that a state of anarchy would bring chaos.

MONARCHY

The oldest form of government is a monarchy. A monarchy is a government that is led by a monarch. A monarch is called different things in different countries: there are kings and queens, emperors and empresses, pharaohs, kaisers and tsars. Monarchies were once common throughout the world, but now they are much rarer.

PASSING ON POWER

The key thing about monarchies is that the leaders do not get elected by the people of the state. Monarchs inherit their power and they rule as they see fit. They get their right to rule from their parents. Most monarchies pass down the male line, meaning that the eldest son inherits the role of king after his father dies or steps down, even if he has older sisters.

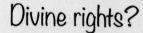

Divine rights?

Early monarchs such as pharaohs who ruled Egypt were believed to get their power from the gods. Later in Europe, some monarchs used this idea to claim the 'divine right of kings', making themselves above any laws men could make. King Louis XIV (1643–1715) of France had no real religious belief in this, but claimed it to try to keep absolute power over his kingdom and the French people.

In monarchies like this, an eldest daughter only inherits the throne when there are no sons, as in the case of Queen Elizabeth II's father George VI. Once in power, monarchs generally reign for the rest of their life.

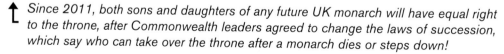

Since 2011, both sons and daughters of any future UK monarch will have equal right to the throne, after Commonwealth leaders agreed to change the laws of succession, which say who can take over the throne after a monarch dies or steps down!

ABSOLUTE MONARCHIES

In an absolute monarchy, the monarch rules with total unlimited power. Some monarchs rule fairly, with the best interests of their people at heart, but others may abuse their power. The kingdom of Swaziland, a small country in southern Africa, is one of the world's last remaining absolute monarchies. The king makes all the laws for the million people in his state, who mainly live in the countryside and follow traditional ways of life. Known as Ngweyama, 'the lion', the king has been criticised for his harsh treatment of opponents and for using public money to pay for new palaces and luxury cars.

MODERN MONARCHIES

Most monarchies today are constitutional monarchies. In a constitutional monarchy, the king or queen is said to be the head of state but they have little real power. There is a government chosen and elected by the people that actually runs the country and makes the laws. The UK, Thailand, the Netherlands and Japan are examples of constitutional monarchies. The Emperor of Japan is the head of the imperial (royal) family and is the ceremonial head of Japan. He is important but he does not have a political function. Instead, he is limited to symbolic roles, such as receiving state guests from other countries and making overseas visits to promote friendships with other countries.

Constitutional monarchs only get to wear crowns and other precious symbols of royal power at very special ceremonies, such as coronations, when they are crowned, or the swearing in of a new leader of an elected government.

THEOCRACY

Theocracy comes from Greek words meaning 'rule by God'. A theocracy is a state that uses the rules of its religion to govern. A true theocracy is a government in which a country is ruled by religious leaders. There are very few absolute theocracies in the world today, but some states are still heavily influenced by the main religion of their country.

VATICAN CITY

The smallest independent state in the world is also the world's only absolute theocracy. Vatican City is a city-state surrounded by Rome in Italy and it is the headquarters of the Roman Catholic Church. The pope acts as leader of the state and governs with a group, or 'college', of cardinals.

Theocratic rulers such as a pope are guided by their religious beliefs and might see themselves as sent by their god to rule their people.

Cardinals are chosen by the pope and they choose one of their own to be a new pope when the old one dies or steps down. Only the cardinals can vote for their new leader and only men can be cardinals, so Vatican City is also the only state in the world where women are not yet allowed to vote in elections.

Ancient Egypt

In ancient times, most states were theocracies. In ancient Egypt, the pharaoh was the most important and powerful person in the kingdom. He was the head of the government and high priest of every temple. He was not just the gods' representative on Earth, but was believed to be a god himself. This meant that what he said came straight from the gods and was therefore law.

MIX AND MATCH

There are several states around the world today that may not be run by a religious leader, but that use religious values as a basis for their laws and other decisions they make. Saudi Arabia is ruled by a royal family, but the state uses a strict type of Islamic law called Sharia, for example that forbids people to worship other religions. The country's constitution is based on the Holy Qur'an (the Muslim holy book). In Iran, even though the president is elected by popular vote, the country's laws are religious laws and the most powerful person is the Supreme Leader, the kingdom's Islamic State's religious leader. He, not the president, controls the armed forces and makes decisions about things like security and defence. He is also the head of radio and TV and confirms the president's election.

The separation of Church and state

Most early states were theocracies. In the 18th century, during a period of time known as the Enlightenment, people in most Western countries decided that instead of religion, states should use science and reason to make rules for governing a state. They thought religion should be a matter of personal choice and that every religion should be protected equally in a country. Today, in most governments around the world religious influence is kept mainly separate from running the state.

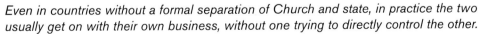

↑ *Even in countries without a formal separation of Church and state, in practice the two usually get on with their own business, without one trying to directly control the other.*

DICTATORSHIP

A dictatorship is a country ruled by a single leader who has full power over the people. Some people might say that's a bit like a classroom ruled over by one teacher, but that would be very unfair! After all a teacher actually asks what you think. In a dictatorship it's best for people to keep their opinions to themselves. If they don't, they could end up in prison, or worse.

ALL FOR ONE AND ONE FOR ALL!

In a dictatorship, one person has total control of the state. They are called a dictator. The dictator has all the power and makes all the laws. A dictator has not been elected and often uses the army to keep control. Dictators may also ban other political parties and lock up or execute anyone who tries to oppose them. They take control of the state's media, its newspapers, radio and TV, to make sure that only their message gets across to the people.

Ancient Rome

The first dictators were in ancient Rome. They were only temporary and were used in an emergency, such as for taking care of rebellions. Rome was ruled by two leaders called consuls, but in a crisis Romans felt it was better to have one person making decisions, so sometimes, one consul became dictator. Dictators could change laws but usually stepped down as soon as the problem was solved.

They ban books that portray other ways of doing things and even make schools teach propaganda, false or exaggerated information that makes the dictator look good.

In a dictatorship, dictators try to make sure that anything that might make them look bad doesn't get seen by their people!

SEIZING CONTROL

Some dictators inherit their power, for example from a parent. Others may resort to force or lying and cheating their way to political power. Dictatorships are also formed when someone takes power suddenly in a coup d'état. A coup d'état is when a small group of people suddenly attack and get rid of an existing government. In this kind of takeover, the new dictator has the support of the police and military to help him or her get to power and when in power the dictator uses these armed forces to stop anyone challenging their new leadership.

There are few dictators today but Alexander Grigoryevich Lukashenko of Belarus, a country in Eastern Europe, is often accused of being one. He has almost total control of government spending and what he says becomes law and the state even owns most of the country's farms.

Fascist dictators

Fascism is when a government is ruled by a dictator who believes that the strength of their country is more important than the well-being of the people. Fascist dictators use harsh controls and authority to control the people's lives and people have few freedoms. The police force and army punish people who disobey and they threaten other countries. Fascist leaders often blame minority groups for a country's problems.

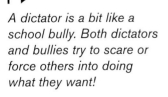

A dictator is a bit like a school bully. Both dictators and bullies try to scare or force others into doing what they want!

TOTALITARIAN STATES

The clue to what this style of government involves is in the name. A totalitarian government is one that tries to keep total control over the lives of all of its citizens. It controls almost every aspect of their everyday lives, both public and private. It is like dictatorship by a party instead of an individual.

ONE PARTY RULE

In a totalitarian state, there is only one political party. This party keeps complete control of the country by not allowing anybody else to form a political party and may brutally punish anyone who disagrees with the government. Citizens are forced to do what the government tells them and may also be prevented from leaving the country. The government may have a say in the job they do, the religion they follow, what they do with their money and even what they watch or read.

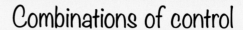

Combinations of control

Many dictatorships are also totalitarian states. Joseph Stalin's Soviet Union (1929 to 1953) and Adolf Hitler's Germany (1933 to 1945) are two of the best-known totalitarian regimes and Stalin and Hitler are two of the most famous fascist dictators.

Under control

Totalitarian governments didn't appear until the twentieth century because the technology needed for controlling large numbers of people did not exist. When television, radio, and other forms of media came along it was easier for a ruling party to take control, often through campaigns of propaganda or by creating a personality cult, where people are constantly told how wonderful their leader is.

A totalitarian state keeps a constant check on its citizens, telling them what to think, what to watch, and even looking at messages they send or receive.

TOTALITARIANISM TODAY

Some people think that China is a totalitarian state because it only has one political party. In fact, China is authoritarian not totalitarian because that party tolerates almost anything except criticism of the party and one-party rule. North Korea is an example of a totalitarian state today. In North Korea the party and state control every aspect of a citizen's life. It is illegal for North Korean people to leave their country without the government's permission, and they need permission from their work unit to even travel to another part of the country.

The government controls the media and if someone reports on you for criticising the party, you and your family 'disappear' from society and end up in a political prison camp. It is illegal to own a radio or use the Internet to get information about the outside world and children have to spend a lot of time learning about, and learning songs that praise, the Kim family that run the state.

In North Korea the totalitarian government even controls people's hairstyles. Women are allowed to choose one of 14 styles and young men have to keep their hair shorter than 5 cm long!

THE DAWN OF DEMOCRACY

Have you ever been to a polling station with your parents on an election day? Or perhaps you've voted for one of your fellow students to represent your class on the school council? If you've ever voted, you've taken part in what we call a democracy.

THE FIRST DEMOCRACY

A democracy is a government system in which people get the chance to say (by voting) how they want their government to be run. This is different from governments such as monarchies or dictatorships in which one ruler makes most of the decisions.

One of the first democracies was in the city-state of Athens, Greece in around 500 BCE. Five hundred citizens were randomly chosen in a lottery to form a government for a year and werepaid a small wage to compensate them for time spent away from their normal jobs.

Unfair forum?

Around 6,000 citizens would meet in the forum (a public square) to vote. Only citizens of Athens could vote and at this time, citizens were only the free, adult men of the city-state. Women, children, foreigners and slaves were not citizens, and could not participate or vote.

Anytime this group wanted to make or change laws, all the citizens of Athens had a chance to vote yes or no during a large meeting called the Assembly, when any citizen could also speak and tell the government what it should be doing!

If people didn't like one of their politicians, oters would scratch or paint his name on a piece of broken pottery and if enough people voted against him in this way, the unwanted candidate could be kicked out of Athens for ten years!

DIRECT DEMOCRACY

The democracy practised in ancient Greece in which all citizens were allowed to vote on every major issue is called direct democracy. Direct democracies may work for smaller groups, but when a country has a large population it would be impossible to hold an election every time a decision had to be made. Elections take months to plan and cost a lot of money. Having a direct democracy would mean every voter would have to read up about every issue to be able to use their vote wisely and take time off work to attend every election. Imagine the time and energy it would take people to learn about every issue facing a country, such as what roads should be built or how long school holidays should be!

Direct democracy works when everyone is voting on a single issue. Or at least it should do …

Referendums

Today, the only time direct democracy is used is when all the citizens vote on a particular issue in a referendum. This is what happened in 2016 when 51.9 per cent of the British people voted in a referendum to leave the European Union. Although 48.1 per cent voted to remain in the European Union, the majority chose to leave so that was the democratic decision that was taken.

DEMOCRACIES TODAY

Most democracies in the world today are representative democracies.
In a representative democracy, voters don't vote on every major issue. Instead, they elect people to represent them to run the government and make those types of decisions.

REPRESENTATIVE DEMOCRACY

A representative democracy is a bit like a school council. School councillors are elected representatives. It is their job to listen to the ideas, suggestions and concerns of the students they represent and make decisions based on what they hear. In a representative democracy, citizens are free to vote for a candidate in their area. When a candidate wins, the political party she or he belongs to also wins. The political party with the maximum number of votes forms the government.

DEMOCRACY'S DOWNSIDES

Democracy isn't perfect. Individuals vote for people who represent their best interests, not necessarily the best interest of others. And after people vote someone into power, they don't really have any control on what that person does, for example if she or he goes back on a promise they made. In some countries, only wealthy people who can afford to put themselves up for election, meaning rich people, hold the real power. And, in countries with only two political parties or groups to choose from, voters have a limited choice of options on some issues.

Some democratic governments have many complicated rules and ways of doing things, which means it can take a long time to reach decisions.

Most countries today are governed by representative democracies (123 out of 192 countries), but there are still differences!

The USA

The United States is a republic because it is headed by one person, the president, who is elected by the people (as opposed to a monarchy ruled by one unelected person). It is a representative democracy because people elect the officials who help to govern their country. It is also a federal government in which power is divided between the federal (or national) government and the 50 states.

India

India is a federal republic in which there is a central government but local governments also have a lot of control. Two leaders share central government power: the Head of State is the president and the head of government is the prime minister. The president has a more ceremonial role and attends political functions, while the prime minister is the leader of the ruling party and runs the government.

Australia

Australia is both a representative democracy and a constitutional monarchy with Queen Elizabeth II as the country's head of state. It is also a federation because powers are divided between a central government and six individual regional governments, which control local matters.

Spain

Spain is a representative democracy that is a constitutional monarchy. The king is head of state, and the prime minister is head of government. The king formally appoints the prime minister.

➡

Despite the problems with democracy, most people living in countries with democratic governments tend to have more freedoms, protections and a higher standard of living than others who do not live in a democracy.

POWER HOUSES

When people think of a government, they usually think of the main building where those in power meet and discuss how to run a country. Inside these houses of power, governments make a lot of important decisions. The way governments come to these decisions is set out in a constitution.

IT'S IN THE CONSTITUTION!

Most modern states have a constitution, a list of rules that define the rights and duties of its citizens and say how a government should work and what issues it can pass laws on. In most democracies, the nation's constitution is written in a single document, such as the United States Constitution. The exceptions are Israel, which uses a set of basic laws as its constitution, and New Zealand and the UK, which have constitutions that have developed over many years and are spread about in a range of legal documents.

A constitution sets out the all-important separation of powers between different levels of government.

New Zealand's main government building is known as the 'Beehive' because of its shape. It has 10 floors above ground and four floors below and is full of government ministers buzzing away at their important jobs.

Seats of power

The main government buildings in any country are known as seats of power. They are usually grand and built in a country's capital or main city. Turkey's Parliament House in Ankara has 16 large chandeliers to represent the country's 16 states. Japan's Tokyo Metropolitan Government Building has two giant towers 243 m tall. It took 17 million bricks and 3,000 people to build India's Rashtrapati Bhavan (Presidential Residence)!

THE SEPARATION OF POWERS

Most democratic governments are divided into three separate sections, or branches: legislative, executive and judicial. The constitution gives each branch different responsibilities, which stops any one of the branches from becoming too powerful. This is known as the separation of powers.

• The executive branch is made up of the government's leader and his or her main elected officials. It is the job of the executive branch to come up with ideas for laws and to make sure that laws and decisions taken by the government are carried out. In countries such as the USA the head of the government is elected directly by the people and in others, such as the UK, the head of the government is the leader of the biggest political party.

• The legislative branch, or legislature, is made up of all the people elected by citizens to work in government on their behalf. These elected representatives have the job of debating and voting on laws proposed by the executive branch.

• The judicial branch, or judiciary, is the justice system of a state and includes the judges, courts and lawyers who interpret and apply the laws on behalf of the state. They make sure that citizens are being treated fairly and justly.

↧ The idea of dividing the work of government into branches is to make the system fairer and stop one person or one group getting hold of too much power.

★ ★ ★ ★ ★ ★ ★ ★ ★ ★ ★ ★ ★ ★

From house to house

In a democracy, each of the three powers usually has its own important, main building. In the USA, these are the White House (executive), Congress (the legislative branch), and the Supreme Court (judiciary).

★ ★ ★ ★ ★ ★ ★ ★ ★ ★ ★ ★ ★ ★

PARLIAMENTARY DEMOCRACIES

Many countries, including Australia, Canada, New Zealand and the UK, are parliamentary democracies. This is where the head of state and head of government are different people and the executive and legislative branches of government are linked.

LINKING TWO BRANCHES

Parliamentary democracies are often constitutional monarchies, where the head of state is a monarch and the head of government is a prime minister. The prime minister is first elected as a member of parliament then elected prime minister by the controlling party in Parliament – the party that got the most votes in the last elections and holds the most seats in government. The prime minister then leads the executive branch of government, which is often known as the Cabinet. As prime minister, she or he is also still part of the legislative branch that makes the laws, and so works directly with other people in Parliament to write and pass laws.

Name that legislature!

Law-making bodies have different names around the world. Australia, Canada, New Zealand and the UK call the legislature the Parliament. Some countries call it the national assembly. In Japan it is the Diet, in Israel the Knesset and in Sweden the Riksdag.

One house or two?

Many countries around the world have only one legislative body including Finland, Israel, New Zealand and Sweden. This is called a unicameral system. ('Uni' means one and 'camera' means chamber in Latin.) Some countries have legislatures that are bicameral: they are spilt into two houses or chambers.

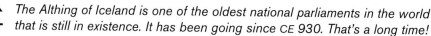

The Althing of Iceland is one of the oldest national parliaments in the world that is still in existence. It has been going since CE 930. That's a long time!

THE HOUSES OF PARLIAMENT

The UK Parliament consists of the House of Lords and the House of Commons. The electorate votes for the Members of the Commons in elections. The country is divided into regions, and people in those regions can vote for a Member of Parliament (MP) to represent them. That's why in the Commons there are members of the government (the controlling party) and members from other parties too. The members of the House of Lords are not elected. Some inherit their status as a lord from their family. Others are appointed for life by the monarch, on the advice of her prime minister. They are chosen because of their achievements or expertise.

In the Commons, the government and opposition members discuss important political ideas, make decisions about how government money should be spent and suggest new laws. The House of Lords debates new laws proposed by the House of Commons, and makes suggestions about changes to those laws. When both Houses finally agree on a law, the Queen approves it and makes it official.

The structure of a democratic state looks like a pyramid. At the bottom are the citizens who vote in elections. When they vote, they elect representatives to a parliament. A government is formed from the members of parliament, usually by the party that has the most seats. At the top is the head of government, the prime minister.

PRESIDENTIAL DEMOCRACIES

In a presidential democracy, the leader is called a president (no surprises there)! She or he is elected by citizens to lead an executive branch of government that is not linked to the legislative branch.

HOW IT WORKS

In a presidential democracy, such as the USA, the president is separate from the legislature. (Remember, in a parliamentary democracy the prime minister is a Member of Parliament and so part of the legislature.) Of course, the president still works with the legislative branch, which is called Congress. The laws that Congress wants to pass must first go through the president. If the president agrees to them then they become official, but the president can also veto (refuse) them.

The two chambers of Congress

The US Congress has two chambers, or houses: the Senate and the House of Representatives. Each of the 50 states that makes up the USA can vote to elect two senators, no matter how big or small the state is, and at least one representative. The more people who live in a state, the more representatives that state is allowed. There are currently 100 senators and 435 representatives.

(Although that veto can be overridden if two-thirds of Congress vote against it.) Likewise, the president can go to the legislative branch and suggest laws, but they ultimately write them for his approval.

➡

The Senate and the House of Representatives that make up Congress work together to pass laws that are then enforced by the executive branch and overseen by the judicial branch.

LIMITING POWER

The idea of having two houses in a law-making body or legislature, whether it is called a parliament or a congress, is that if one area of government tries to overstep its limits, the other can correct it. For example, a US president can only spend money if a budget is approved by Congress and if a president tried to declare war on another country Congress could take steps to stop it. The powers of the second house or chamber vary. In many countries, such as the UK, the upper house has a limited power of veto. In Australia, the upper house has full power of veto, which means it can block whatever laws it does not like.

The president and both houses of Congress must approve a bill before it becomes a law. Some bills are revised many times before everyone agrees.

France's halfway house

France has a combination of a presidential and parliamentary system! The president functions as the head of the state and is elected by the people. As the head of state, the president controls foreign policy and defence, and appoints a prime minister with the approval of Parliament.

The prime minister acts as the head of government and is in charge of domestic policy (decisions about things that only affect France). The Parliament, made up of the Senate and the National Assembly, creates and votes on laws.

WHAT GOVERNMENTS DO

Look around you. What do you see? Shelves of books, computers on desks or a busy teacher in your classroom? A street with traffic lights or a park full of trees? Perhaps a rubbish lorry emptying bins? These things and places and many of the people at work in them are all there because of governments.

PUBLIC SERVICES

Providing public services is a key task for governments. You can probably guess that public service means supplying things to the public. The government is in charge of creating infrastructure, the basic equipment and structures such as buildings, roads and power supplies that a country needs to function properly. It provides state schools and the equipment in them and pays teachers to teach children who attend school. It even decides stuff like what gets taught and how many children are in your class. Governments help to provide hospitals and doctors and other healthcare staff who help people when they are sick and decide how much it costs to buy prescription medicines.

Providing services

Governments face challenges when providing public services. For example, as people live longer because of better healthcare, they will need more healthcare and this will require more money. Governments have to decide where that money comes from and what level of public services they will provide.

Other public services include the fire service, police forces and the armed forces that defend a country.

→

The kind and quality of public services a government provides depends on where you live in the world.

LAW AND ORDER

One of the most basic duties of a government is to protect its people. The government protects people from other citizens who may harm them, steal from them or damage their property by making laws that are enforced by the police.

A law exists because most of the people in a country agree and to look after the health or safety of everyone in a country. Laws tell people what they must do and what they cannot do. There are laws that say people must wear seatbelts in a car and that children should go to school. There are laws that stop people speeding or taking something that does not belong to them. Laws apply to everyone and anyone can be punished if they break a law. The law also protects people from being punished if they haven't done anything wrong.

New laws

To make a new law in the UK, a Member of Parliament (MP) makes a suggestion to the other MPs in Parliament. Their draft – or proposed – law is called a bill. It must be discussed in the House of Commons and in the House of Lords. When this is done and if the new law is agreed, the Queen must give her approval. The bill then becomes an act, which means it becomes a law.

Laws are there to help society work smoothly. Take traffic lights as an example. When people obey traffic lights, people get to work and school quickly and safely. If every driver just did what they wanted at every crossroads, chaos would ensue!

THE ECONOMY

The economy is the way a government manages its money and resources to produce, buy and sell goods and services. Resources are things like land or coal. Goods are products like cars, food or clothes, and services are ways people help or serve each other, for example teaching, building or hairdressing. Governments aim for their country to produce more goods and services each year so that its people are better off. When there is more demand for goods and services, businesses have more work and provide more people with jobs and wages. When businesses do well they also pay more tax to governments.

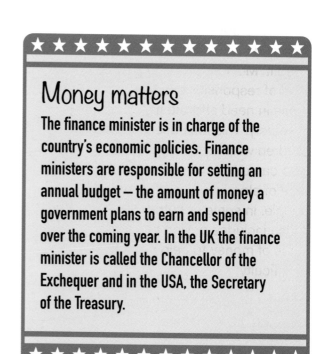
GOVERNMENT INTERVENTION

Governments do a variety of things to help businesses be successful. For example, they might give loans or payments to help farmers grow more food or to help them recover after a disaster like a flood Governments may help businesses by training and paying for mentors, people with business experience who give help and advice to people starting or expanding companies.

 Governments are also in charge of printing and regulating money.

WELFARE AND ASSISTANCE

Welfare is government-provided help and support for people who need it. Most governments take some level of responsibility for helping those in need and the most vulnerable in society. This includes looking after children who have no parents or family who can care for them and taking care of elderly, sick and disabled people. In some countries it also includes paying benefits, sums of money to help people in difficulty.

This might include paying money to someone who has lost their job or earns a low wage, paying a hostel to take care of homeless people or paying someone who needs to stay at home to look after a relative. State benefits are things that everyone can benefit from, but there are rules about who can get them and there are government departments and workers who check if someone is eligible for help.

★ ★ ★ ★ ★ ★ ★ ★ ★ ★ ★

Time for taxes

The things that a government provides are not free. To pay for all the things they have to do, from paying wages to people who provide services to paying for roads to be mended, parks to be tended or traffic lights to work, governments collect taxes. Taxes are an amount of money that a government requires people to pay according to things like how much they earn and how much the house they own is worth.

★ ★ ★ ★ ★ ★ ★ ★ ★ ★ ★

↑ *Most governments take several different kinds of taxes from their people. Road tax is money car owners have to pay for driving on the roads and the money raised is used to maintain the road network.*

THE ENVIRONMENT

When you go for a walk in woodland or swim in the sea or a river, you probably don't give a thought to who protects these wild places and the animals that live there. But as populations grow and there is more demand for land to build more houses and grow more food, wild places and habitats are under threat. Governments have responsibility for protecting the environment.

ENVIRONMENTAL PROTECTION

One way in which governments protect the environment is by making and enforcing laws that keep air and water clean and paying scientists to study levels of pollution around us. Governments also create protected areas, such as national parks, where nature and wildlife are protected and where people can continue to enjoy nature without destroying it.

Governments also protect habitats and wildlife by preventing people from building or clearing all of a country's green spaces and by making laws to stop people harming wild animals, by buying and selling rare and protected animals for example.

Natural disasters

Our environment provides us with many resources but it can also cause trouble, for example when a natural disaster such as a flood hits. Governments help communities avoid or recover from flooding and other weather-related hazards. They make studies of where these events might happen and what effects they might have so they can make plans about how to prevent them or help people if they occur.

→

Some governments make trucks with special filters hat reduce the exhaust fumes that they pump out into the air to make air safer for us to breathe.

LOCAL GOVERNMENT

Local governments or city governments are the group of politicians who run services within their areas and try to improve what is already available. For example, they look after the roads in their area and fund new cycle tracks. They are responsible for local schools and local housing, for helping homeless people and making decisions about where new houses should be built. They organise rubbish collection and recycling and run campaigns encouraging people to do more to reduce and recycle their waste.

Local governments usually get most of their money from central government and the rest they get from local taxes. There are some things local governments have to do, such as clean the streets, and other things that they do if they want to or have enough money, like put on fireworks displays or street festivals. Councillors have to answer to the local people who elect them and represent their local communities in major decisions that will affect their areas.

Councils and mayors

Many local governments are called councils and are made up of councillors elected by the people and paid officials. Many city councils also have an elected mayor. The mayor leads the council but decisions are made by the whole council. Most councillors are representatives of a political party.

↑ *Some mayors get involved in organising major sports and music events in their area.*

FOREIGN AFFAIRS

Being on good terms with other countries is an important part of any government's job because it can stop disagreements that can lead to conflicts and wars. Different governments also work with each other in order to come to agreements about how their countries' businesses can buy and sell goods to and from each other. Trade agreements cover things like working out reduced tariffs, taxes that are applied only to goods or services that are imported, or brought into a country from another country to sell.

EMBASSIES AND DIPLOMATS

There is so much interaction between countries in today's world that governments send representatives to live and work in different countries. An embassy is a group of diplomats who represent their country in a foreign country and also the name of the building where they work. The embassy building is usually in the capital city of the foreign country.

Diplomats try to make relations between countries run as smoothly as possible and help any of their country's citizens abroad. The ambassador is the highest official in an embassy and spokesperson for the home government.

Diplomats have sometimes been accused of spying on the country they work in, trying to find out state secrets that could help their own government back home.

★ ★ ★ ★ ★ ★ ★ ★ ★ ★ ★ ★ ★ ★ ★ ★ ★

Protecting diplomats

There are rules that diplomats cannot be arrested by the police in the foreign country where they work for any crime and that the host country should do all they can to protect the ambassador and diplomats working there. Most countries consider any attack on an embassy as an attack on the country it represents.

★ ★ ★ ★ ★ ★ ★ ★ ★ ★ ★ ★ ★ ★ ★ ★ ★

INTERNATIONAL COOPERATION

Governments from different countries also form and join special groups and organisations to tackle big issues that cross borders. These organisations are a bit like clubs. To join, a country has to agree to follow the rules and may have to pay a fee. In return they get certain benefits. For example, the European Union is a group of countries in Europe whose governments work together to do things like help people earn enough money, receive fair treatment and live in safety without the threat of war.

➡

The United Nations logo contains a map of the world that represents all the people and the countries of the world, surrounded by olive branches, which are a symbol for peace.

THE UNITED NATIONS

One of the biggest and most important international organisations is the United Nations. The UN was formed in 1945 after the Second World War (1939–1945), to prevent more world wars. Today it is made up of 193 countries and has different sections that work on different projects. The UN organises peace-keeping forces in trouble spots around the world. It helps refugees and looks after the needs of children. It strives to combat diseases and health problems globally and works to end world hunger by helping to improve farming and fishing practices.

Super summits

Summits are events where leaders or diplomats from different countries meet to discuss a shared problem. Governments of the world organise summits to tackle important issues such as a threat of war or climate change.

At climate change summits, governments of countries around the world set targets for reducing energy use that contributes to global warming.

POLITICAL IDEAS

Have you ever heard politicians from different parties arguing on the radio or TV? Political parties argue because they have different ideas about how to run a country. People often describe these ideas as left wing and right wing, or socialism and conservatism. Most countries have more than two parties, which may be more or less left or right wing, or nearer the centre of the two.

ON THE RIGHT

There's a range of right-wing parties and they all have slightly different ideas, but in general conservatism is based on conserving, or keeping, systems as they are and avoiding too many changes. Right-wing politicians tend to believe that it is natural that some people in society are better off than others as this gives people the ability to achieve and succeed. Most also think that it's up to individuals to look after themselves and that in most cases charities, churches, and communities should help people in need, not the government. Right-wing politicians may also believe in using strict laws to protect society and its traditions and in using strong penalties to punish criminals.

Right-wing parties

The main right-wing political parties in a country have different names around the world.

Australia: Liberal Party of Australia
Germany: Christian Democrat Union of Germany
France: The Republicans
UK: The Conservative (or Tory) Party
USA: The Republican Party

↑ *In many government buildings, left-wing parties often sit on the left and right-wing parties sit on the right!*

MONEY, MONEY, MONEY

Right-wing thinkers believe that businesses should be privately owned and that the government should not try to put controls on private companies. They think that having more freedom allows businesses to earn more money and that this should benefit a country. They also believe in keeping the taxes that people pay to the government low, so people can keep as much of what they earn as possible. This means a government has less to spend on helping people or paying for things like a health service, but right-wing politicians believe that when people pay less tax they have more money to spend on the private services they want. So, for example, they might choose to pay for private health insurance to pay for their doctors and health care if they get ill.

Natural disasters

When people talk about the far right, they mean extreme right-wing ideas. For example, many far-right groups and parties think that their government should not pay for any systems that help people in need or people they consider foreigners. Some are also anti-immigration, which means they don't want any people from other countries living in theirs.

⬆ *Most right-wing and left-wing parties today don't really stick to just right-wing or left-wing policies, but instead lean towards a 'middle ground', in order to win over potential voters!*

ON THE LEFT

Left-wing political parties all have different ideas, but in general socialism is based on the theory that people are social creatures who live together in communities. People on the left tend to believe that governments should help people work together rather than compete with each other.

THE ROLE OF GOVERNMENT

Left-wing politicians believe that government should play a larger role in people's lives than conservatives do. They think that wealth should be spread more evenly in order for all people to be treated fairly and that governments should have more controls over private businesses to make things better for everyone. For example, they might be more likely to call for an increase in the minimum wage, the lowest hourly amount a worker can be paid.

Some socialists or left-wing thinkers believe that the state should run some key industries that affect everyone, such as the railways …

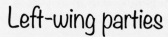

Left-wing parties

The main left-wing political parties in a country have different names around the world.

Australia: The Australian Labor party
Germany: Social Democratic Party of Germany
France: The Socialist Party
UK: The Labour Party
USA: The Democrat Party

This means workers get a bigger share of the company's profits. Many also think that the state should own some of a country's most important industries, such as the water industry or the railways. By doing so, they can make sure those industries work for everyone and that the whole country can benefit from the profits those industries make.

HIGHER TAXES, MORE SERVICES

Many left-wing politicians believe that there should be different levels of tax depending on how much people earn. The idea is that the more someone earns, the more they should pay. Then the government can use the extra money to provide services for everybody, rich and poor. So, for example, a government could use the extra money to improve public services such as healthcare and education that are free for everyone to use. They could also use it to specifically help people who are poorer or less fortunate, for example by paying for places for homeless people to stay or to help people who are out of work. They believe that a good welfare system means people are healthier and more able to work, and so will be able to put more back into the economy.

Liberalism

Liberalism is a sort of middle way between left-wing and right-wing ideas. Liberals believe that the government should provide support for people who need it but also that it should help people to help themselves. They think that governments should step in as much as is needed, for example to have some controls on business, but that people and businesses should also be free to make money for themselves.

Neither right- or left-wing ideas are 'wrong'. It is just a matter of perspective, and both have been designed with the best of intentions. Most people find that they agree with some policies and disagree with others regardless of whether they are left- or right-wing.

MAKING MONEY

One of the main things politicians argue about is the economy: how money is earned and used within a country. Communism and capitalism are two opposite ways of dealing with the way money and the economy work in a country.

HOW COMMUNISM WORKS

Communism is the belief that everything in a state, including money, should be shared out equally between people. This means that all property and businesses, such as mines, factories and farms, are owned by the people and wealth is shared equally between people or according to their needs, whatever their abilities are. In theory, communism should mean that there is no poverty in a country. The problem is that in order to keep control, communist leaders in the past, such as Stalin in the Soviet Union, and Mao Zedong in China, used cruel measures to suppress opposition and enforce their ideas. So, in the end people rejected them. At one time, about one-third of the world's population lived under communist governments. Today, there are just five communist states: China, Cuba, Laos, North Korea and Vietnam.

↑ *People say that the problems with communism are that people are not free to make their own choices and decisions and that there is no incentive to work or try hard because everyone gets the same rewards anyway!*

HOW CAPITALISM WORKS

Capitalism promotes private ownership of property and businesses, such as factories, offices and transport companies, to create capital (money). In capitalism, buyers influence the market through what they choose to buy and how much they can spend on goods and services. Businesses care about making money, so they create whatever goods people will buy. The idea is that business runs the economy and the government stays out of it. Capitalism is also described as free market economy or free enterprise, because people and businesses are free to earn and spend their money as they wish. One problem with capitalism is that some people make more money than others and gradually a gap can grow between rich people who own big businesses and people who work for them, who may remain poor.

MIXED ECONOMIES

Neither capitalism nor communism are perfect in their pure forms, so many governments are experimenting with mixed economies. Mixed economies are those that use welfare capitalism or liberalism. They basically follow a capitalist model but the government also uses rules and controls to ensure that workers are not pushed into poverty.

In a capitalist economy, the government pays for any services it provides, like education, by taking money from people's earnings in the form of taxes.

HOW ELECTIONS WORK

Voting is a way for a group of people to make a fair decision. Maybe you've had a family vote about where to go on holiday or have been involved in a school vote about uniforms. When people vote to give a person or political party power, it's called an election. Elections are important because they are when people get to have a say in how they are governed.

DIFFERENT ELECTIONS

There are different kinds of elections. In some places people get to vote on who should lead local governments, which affect what happens in their immediate area. They might get a say in jobs and industries that come to an area, water services, road repair or rubbish collection, for example. Local politicians can also take concerns of people in their local area to politicians at a national level, who have more power and access to more funds. For example, they might be able to help a region create more jobs by offering local companies grants, money to start up or expand. In a general election people get to choose presidents, prime ministers and the political parties that run entire countries.

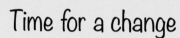

Time for a change

Most democratic countries have regular general elections, when the people get to vote to keep the current government or choose a new one to run things. The UK holds a general election at least once every five years. An election for the President of the United States occurs every four years.

↑ *Elected governments usually get four or five years to put their ideas into action. After that, people get a chance to decide if they are working, and if not to replace the old government with a new one.*

Voting matters because by voting, you get to say what's important to you, and you say it straight to the politicians. Even if the party or person you vote for loses, your vote lets people know who supports their points of view.

PARTY TIME!

Before people head to the polling station, where they vote, they find out what the different politicians and parties running for election are all about. Politicians with similar beliefs about how a government should work form political parties and come up with policies, which are ideas and proposals about how to run a country. For instance, some parties might focus on the environment and have lots of ideas about how to tackle climate change. Others might focus on crime and what new laws they would bring in to reduce it. Politicians also carry out polls, which are special surveys, to find out what people want and to help them formulate their plans. When political parties have a plan, they set about persuading people to vote for them and their policies in an election.

Make your vote count

In some countries a higher proportion of older people turn out to vote than younger voters aged 18-24. Politicians want votes so they notice this stuff. Statistics like this might encourage politicians to spend more time and effort on issues that are important to older people, like pensions. If younger voters don't vote in higher numbers politicians may pay less attention to issues that are important to young people, such as university fees or climate change.

MAKING CHOICES

You wouldn't choose a new phone without finding out what it could do for you, would you? No! And voters shouldn't choose to elect a leader or a political party without knowing what they stand for either.

VOTING MATTERS

So, how can people find out what different political parties stand for and what they would do in government? Political parties and candidates publish plans and promises in manifestos, which anyone can read. They also have large teams of people working for them who try to convince voters to vote for them. The teams study polls and statistics to work out what matters to voters and try to say and do the right things to get elected. Politicians run adverts on TV, distribute leaflets and posters, go door to door to meet voters, have debates with each other, make speeches and try lots of other ways to persuade voters they are the best choice.

↑ *When it comes to your turn to vote in an election, be informed and read a variety of newspapers and reports so that you can make up your own mind, rather than have it made up for you.*

Beware of bias

Watching political debates and reading manifestos helps people make an informed choice. If people only read newspapers or other people's opinions, they might not make the right choice for them. Many newspapers have a right-wing or left-wing bias and interpret facts in different ways because of those beliefs.

Imagine if the rich owner of a newspaper didn't want people to get higher wages because that would affect their profits. Do you think they might try to persuade readers to vote for a party that did not raise the minimum wage?

AT THE POLLING STATION

When election day arrives, people head down to their local polling station. This is often in a local school or sports centre. At the local polling station, there are people with a list of all of the registered voters in that area. They cross names off their list when each people comes to vote. This ensures no one votes more than once or tries to vote under someone else's name.

They give voters a ballot paper or card, which has a list of candidates on it with boxes next to the names. The voter goes to a private booth where they make a mark, usually an 'X', next to the candidates they want to vote for. Then they fold the ballot paper and put it into a ballot box. A ballot box is a temporarily sealed container with a narrow slot in the top. Ballot boxes are designed to stop anyone from looking at the votes until the polls have closed – the end of the voting period – when they are officially opened and the votes counted.

The secret ballot is designed to stop people being influenced by others when they vote. It doesn't mean you have to go to the polling station in disguise!

★ ★ ★ ★ ★ ★ ★ ★ ★ ★ ★ ★ ★ ★ ★ ★ ★ ★

Who can vote?

In most places in the world, all citizens of a country (who were born or live permanently there) who are over the age of 18 or 21 have the right to vote in elections. It wasn't always that way. Black men and women did not get the right to vote in South African elections until 1994 and women in Saudi Arabia only voted for the first time in general elections in 2015.

★ ★ ★ ★ ★ ★ ★ ★ ★ ★ ★ ★ ★ ★ ★ ★ ★ ★

COUNTING THE VOTES

Election results are not all counted up in the same way. There are different electoral or voting systems to decide who wins. There are three main kinds, but countries may use different ones for different types of elections and some countries use a mixture of all three!

FIRST PAST THE POST

In some systems, the winner is the candidate who receives the most votes in an election. It doesn't matter whether or not more than half of the voters choose them, so long as they have a larger number of votes than other candidates.

The US electoral college

In the US, there is a system called the 'electoral college'. Each state is allocated a certain number of electors, based on their population. States with the most people have the most electors. The candidate who gets the most votes in a state usually gets all of that state's electoral votes. A candidate must win more than half the electoral votes to become president. It is possible for a candidate to win the popular vote nationwide but still lose the electoral college vote.

The UK, Canada, India, the USA and many other countries use the first past the post voting (FPP). People only vote for one candidate and the winning candidate is the one who gains more votes than any other.

➡
In the UK's first past the post system, the candidate with the most votes in each constituency wins and becomes the MP for that seat. All other votes are disregarded, even if it was a photo finish!

MAJORITY SYSTEMS

In majority electoral systems candidates need an absolute majority of 51 per cent of votes or more to win. In the Australian AV (alternative vote) system, voters rank candidates in order of preference, say 1–5. If no first choice candidate gets a majority, the candidate with the lowest number of votes is dropped and the second preferences of that candidate's supporters are distributed. This goes on until one candidate gets an absolute majority. France has a two round system, or TRS. If no candidate wins an absolute majority of votes in the first round, the winner is elected by a second ballot. This is a contest between the two biggest vote winners or those who got over a certain percentage of the votes.

Every vote counts. Even though it can seem as if one vote cannot make much of a difference, some elections can come down to just a few votes so a few could help swing a vote.

PROPORTIONAL REPRESENTATION

In proportional representation voting systems a party wins the same number of seats in government as the share of votes they got. In the closed list system, each political party makes a list of their candidates, ranked in order. A party that wins 30 pre cent of the votes gets 30 per cent of the seats. They give these seats to their politicians, working their way down their list. This system is used by many countries in Western Europe.

Coalitions
In countries with a lot of political parties, none may win enough votes to win an election on its own. So, two or more parties may form a coalition or alliance to become the government.

HOW TO WIN AN ELECTION

Can you imagine the excitement of winning an election and being made leader of a whole country? You may not be able to put yourself forward to run for prime minister or president just yet, but you can try to win an election!

SCHOOL COUNCILS

Have you ever thought about joining a school council? Think about all of the decisions that are made about your school. A school council is a group of students elected by other pupils to represent their views and work with head teachers and governors to improve a school. They provide a way for pupils to discuss issues and make decisions which can help everyone in school. School councils get involved in things like schemes to stop bullying or to fund new playground equipment. Sometimes they even get involved in interviewing new teachers. In most schools, every class elects two representatives, one girl and one boy, to be members of the school council every year. The representatives from all the classes form a council, which is a bit like a government.

How school councils work

After a school council has been elected, it may meet to choose officers. These may include a chairperson to run the meetings, a secretary to take notes at meetings and a treasurer to look after any money that the school council is allocated. In a larger school there may be separate year councils, with a large meeting of the whole school council once a term.

↑ *You could get involved in an election for school councillors or when a school has a vote on a single issue, such as banning school uniforms.*

BECOMING A CANDIDATE

Before you put yourself forward as a candidate in a school election, think about whether you want to do it for the right reasons. Are you doing it just to be popular or to impress teachers or parents? The real reasons for going on a school council are to make your school a better place, to make your voice heard and to make a difference. In some classes, people can just tell their teacher they want to be a candidate. In others, you may need two nominees, pupils who say they support you and it is perfectly okay to ask people to nominate you.

You may feel nervous about putting yourself up for election but it is exciting to see what happens when people share their ideas so go for it! Try to picture how it will feel to win and how you'll feel if you don't at least give it a try.

★ ★ ★ ★ ★ ★ ★ ★ ★ ★ ★ ★ ★ ★ ★

The right to be heard

For many years, people thought it was best for adults to make all the decisions about children, but adults didn't always make the right decisions. So, when countries of the world agreed on a set of children's rights called the Convention on the Rights of Children, they included the right for children to be involved in decisions that affect them and to have their opinions taken into account. One way to do this is in a school council.

★ ★ ★ ★ ★ ★ ★ ★ ★ ★ ★ ★ ★ ★ ★

Even if you are nervous, imagine what you could achieve if you win an election and get a chance to make positive changes at your school. This should give you the courage to put yourself forward. (Just try to keep your aims realistic!)

VOTE FOR ME!

So, you've been accepted as a candidate for a school election. What's next? What can you do to stand out from the other candidates and win those all-important votes?

MEET THE VOTERS

First things first. You may have brilliant ideas about what needs doing, but do other students agree? You need to find out what issues matter to them. You can do this by chatting to as many people as you can, or by devising a questionnaire for students to fill in. You could ask open questions such as 'How can our school be improved?' and some directed questions, such as 'How can we improve the lunch menu?' or 'What can we do to reduce bullying?' Speaking to people you don't know can be scary, but it gets easier with practise.

Make an impact!

There are lots of ways to make sure people hear about you and your ideas. You could design a campaign leaflet, poster or even create a website. Try to keep your message clear and maybe choose a slogan. A slogan is a short, catchy and easy to remember phrase, such as 'When you want something done, Jess is the one'. Let people know who you are and that you mean business!

Start off by smiling and introducing yourself. Explain why you want to ask a few questions. Listen to what people say, make a note of their suggestions and don't forget to say thank you!

To win votes, you need more than good ideas. You also need to be able to get those good ideas across to the people who might vote for you!

SPEAK UP!

Giving a speech is a great chance to tell people why they should vote for you. The secret to success is to be prepared. Take time to write a good speech. In it you could introduce yourself and say why you are a candidate. Talk about the issues people told you matter to them and how you plan to make a difference. Keep the speech short, simple and strong. Use an opening that catches their attention and an ending to keep them talking about you. Check and rewrite it until it's great. Make it clear why people should vote for you. When it's time to give your speech, try to look at the audience and talk directly to them. Speak clearly and with confidence to show you really believe what you say.

Once you're happy with your speech, write it on note cards. Practise it lots of times until you can remember most of it and only need the note cards as back-up. Practise it in front of the mirror, then in front of friends and family and ask them for (useful!) feedback.

★ ★ ★ ★ ★ ★ ★ ★ ★ ★ ★ ★ ★ ★ ★ ★ ★

Lead by example
Look at politicians in power today and from the past too. What makes them special? Watch their speeches to see how they speak clearly and concisely and how they connect with their audiences.

★ ★ ★ ★ ★ ★ ★ ★ ★ ★ ★ ★ ★ ★ ★ ★ ★

Successful candidates have great teams working with them so ask your friends to help you. They could help to pin your posters up around school and encourage others to vote for you.

GETTING RESULTS

It's just as important that elections are fair and well-organised in a school as it is in a general election. And the work doesn't stop once the election is over and the results are in. That's when you get the chance to put plans into action!

It's important that pupils know when and how to vote and take their chance to pick the candidate that they believe will represent them best.

MAKING ELECTIONS WORK

For an election to be fair, the whole school should be notified that it is going to happen and when it will happen. This should happen in advance so people can think about their choices. It could be in the form of a poster or an announcement in assembly for example. Some schools just give every pupil a ballot card. Others require students to register to vote, like they would have to do in a general election and each registered voter gets a card and a number that is noted when they vote.

The ballot papers should be printed with candidate names and space to make a cross by one of them. A teacher or group of students may sit at a table to check their registration lists and who votes. Voting should be in secret and pupils reassured that they do not have to tell anyone who they voted for. When everyone has voted, the ballot boxes are collected and votes counted. The newly elected representatives or school council members may be announced at a special assembly.

GETTING TO WORK

The real work starts after the election is over and you are successful. School councillors are elected by the pupils in their class to attend school council meetings. There you will take part in discussions about plans for the school, share the views and ideas of your classmates with other members of the school council and report back to the class about what was discussed at meetings and what happened about their suggestions.

Try to be proactive in your new role. That means not just waiting for other people to come up with ideas but talking with your class about ideas for projects to improve your school that you can take to the council. School councils have set up all sorts of different projects. They have set up fundraising events and links with local businesses to pay for improvements to their school grounds such as a new play area or building an outside classroom for use by school clubs.

➡
Communication is key. You can make sure there are different ways for people to tell you their ideas, for example in class time, suggestion boxes or questionnaires.

Taking a lead

As well as getting new stuff for their school, some councils get involved in improving life in a school. For example, councils who raise funds to purchase new playground equipment may put in place rules to prevent it from being damaged, such as banning pupils from using the new equipment if they break the rules.

POWER TO THE PEOPLE

When 19th century US president Abraham Lincoln gave one of his most famous speeches in 1863, he spoke of 'government of the people, by the people, for the people'. This means that ordinary people should be able to join governments, that people should choose their own governments and that governments should do what is best for the people of their country. In most modern democratic governments this puts power firmly in the hands of the people!

RIGHTS AND RESPONSIBILITIES

When people vote for a government and give them the right to rule a country, people also agree to take some responsibility for the success of that government. When we choose a government to uphold our rights, such as our right to live in safety, we also have responsibilities. Those responsibilities can include agreeing to pay taxes and obey laws. Children have the right to an education and governments and teachers have a responsibility to provide it for them, but children also have the responsibility to follow school rules and not to disrupt lessons or distract classmates from their education. Sometimes, we agree to laws or rules that could be said to restrict some of our rights, in order to do the right thing. For example, road laws give people no choice about whether or not to wear seat belts, but they do so to save lives.

Wherever there are rights, there are responsibilities. One cannot exist without the other. It's about balance.

TAKING PART

During the build-up to an election and even after a government has been elected, ordinary people can have a say in how it works. Of course, the more people are involved in a campaign, the more attention politicians will pay to it. That's why people get together to organise marches or sign petitions to take to their governments to let them know what they want and how politicians can help them. To get more people interested in joining a campaign, publicity is needed. That's why some groups try to get a celebrity or film star involved, because they always attract media attention. Once an issue is on TV or the Internet there is a greater chance more people will get involved.

The government is a little like the management of the country. If a restaurant isn't up to scratch you might complain to the manager, so if something your government does isn't right, then you should be able to complain to them too!

There are lots of ways people can take part in government. One is to collect signatures on a petition supporting an idea for change.

Have a say

There are lots of ways ordinary people can have a say in what a government does. For example, if the government is talking about bringing in a law that someone disagrees with, they can get in touch with their local Member of Parliament, senator or other official that represents their area to ask them to vote or campaign against it. They can also contact elected officials to ask them to bring a particular issue to the attention of the government.

YOUR VOTE MATTERS

Voting is important because for most of the people in a country, voting is the main way they can influence decisions about how their country is run. The outcome of an election could change your life, so why wouldn't you want to get involved?

BE INFORMED

To make your vote count, it's vital to have an opinion, to know what you think about different issues and what you think of the different political parties' ideas for tackling those issues. Lots of people are influenced by what their parents think and that is fine. But it is good to take some time to develop your own opinions too. You could read more news reports or watch more news programmes on television to keep up-to-date with what is going on in the world of politics.

When people feel strongly about an issue this can spark heated arguments, but it's by talking things through that we work out solutions to the problems or challenges we face.

Talk about it

If you have ideas about an issue that matters to you, talk about it. Other people might not agree with you, but that's fine. It's important for friends, classmates and adults to value each other's opinions and talk to each other in a friendly way about things that matter.

You could also work out what big issues matter most to you and find out more about what can be done about it. For example, if you are particularly interested in the environment and the effects of something like climate change or rainforest deforestation, you might want to find out what different parties are doing about those issues.

BE POSITIVE

Some people get fed up with all the fuss that comes with an election, when politicians seem to be everywhere you look. Some people get annoyed with political parties who bad-mouth people in the other political parties rather than talk about the positive things they will do to bring about changes and improvements. Try not to let these things put you off. Most of the people who go into politics do so because they care about their society and feel like they have positive ideas about how to make it better. There are politicians out there who share your beliefs and ideals and who, if you and enough people vote for them, will put them into practice.

MAKE A DIFFERENCE

Politics is a part of all our lives now, at this very moment. If you're interested, there are many ways you can get involved and take action to make a difference. Think about what you could do. Just as one vote can make a difference when put together with other votes, small actions can add up to a big difference. So, if you're concerned about the environment, you could help your family or school reduce pollution, perhaps by encouraging people to walk or cycle to school or reducing the amount of waste they send to landfill. One day, maybe your experience in working on issues that you'd like to change might lead you into taking an even more active role in your country's government too.

↑ *What issues matter to you? Who will you vote for and how will you make a difference in the future?*

QUIZ

1 If an alien knocked on your door and asked to speak to your leader, would you take them to see:
  a Your teacher
  b Your country's government
  c Your parents

2 Which of these is the correct definition of a government?
  a The bunch of people who tell everyone what to do
  b The group of people who are elected to help run a country
  c The king or queen and royal family

3 How do kings, queens and other monarchs generally come to power?
  a Citizens vote for them in an election
  b They inherit their title from their parents or family
  c They ask nicely

4 What is a democracy?
  a A government that uses a religion's rules to govern
  b A system of government in which the people choose leaders by voting for them
  c A government ruled by a dictator who ws not elected by the people

5 Where was the world's most famous first democracy?
  a Iceland, in around CE 930
  b Athens, Greece, in around 500 BCE
  c The North Pole, last week

6 Many governments are divided into three separate sections or branches called:
  a The legislature, the executive and the referendum
  b The legislature, the executive and the judiciary
  c The legislature, the executive and the dictatorship

7 Which of these statements is false?
  a The United States is a republic
  b France is a theocracy
  c The United Kingdom is a constitutional monarchy

8 What are the names of the two houses that make up the British Parliament?
  a The House of Ladies and the House of Commons
  b The House of Lords and the House of Commons
  c The House of Lords and the House of Constitutions

9 What is an MP?
  a A Man of the People
  b A Member of Parliament
  c A Master of Parliament

10 Which of the following is NOT an example of what the taxes people pay are used for?
  a To pay for public services such as fire services and health services
  b To buy skateboards for MPs to ride to work
  c To pay government workers and ministers to run the country

11 Which of these statements best describe a Communist system of government?
  a The belief that businesses and people should be free to earn and spend their money as they wish
  b The belief that everything in a state should be shared equally between its people
  c The belief that people don't need a government to rule over them

12 How often does a UK government hold a general election?
  a Every year
  b At least once every five years
  c Whenever a leader feels like it

13 What is the best way to learn about a political party's ideas?
  a Read one newspaper's opinion pieces
  b Read the political party's manifesto and their website
  c Phone a friend

14 Why is it important to vote when you get the chance?
  a Going to the polling station is a chance to meet up with friends and neighbours
  b Voting is the way we decide who will be the best people to make decisions for us
  c It's not important to vote

ANSWERS

Mostly Bs
Congratulations! You have a great understanding of how politics works, how it affects us and why we vote. Now you know the basics, spread the word. Tell your friends how interesting politics can be and how important it is to get involved. Perhaps you might consider joining a school council, or getting involved in local, national or even international politics and decision-making. You and our friends are the future and it is time to make your voices and ideas heard!

Mostly As and Cs
Oh dear… it seems that you wouldn't know the difference between a dictator and a dinner lady! Perhaps you need to read the book again? After all, governments make decisions that affect nearly every aspect of our lives, every day. The world of politics can be fascinating and is so important – it is really worth getting to grips with the basics so you can be an informed citizen and have a positive impact on your future and the future of everyone around you.

GLOSSARY

border boundary separating two countries

budget an amount of money available for spending that is based on a plan for how it will be spent

campaign a series of actions or events that are meant to achieve a particular result, such as an election campaign

candidate a person who competes to be elected to government (or any other job)

citizen a person who legally belongs to a country and has the rights and protection of that country

civil war a war between citizens of the same country

climate change changes in the world's weather patterns

community a group of people living in the same place or having a particular characteristic in common

constitution the system of beliefs and laws by which a government runs a country or state

constitutional monarchy system of government as used in the UK where a king or queen is head of state but a government chosen and elected by the people runs the country and makes the laws.

debate a serious, often public, discussion about important issues

diplomat an official representing a country abroad

eligible able or qualified to be chosen for something

environment the air, water, and land in or on which people, animals, and plants live

executive an executive branch of a government comes up with ideas for laws and makes sure that laws and decisions taken by the government are carried out

federal government a system that divides up power between a strong national government and smaller local governments

global warming the gradual increase in the Earth's average temperature

govern to rule or run a country

government the people in power, the people given authority over other people

habitat a place or type of place where a group of plants and animals lives

inherit to receive money, a house, or a title such as king or queen from someone after they have died

judiciary the justice system of a state or country that includes the judges, courts and lawyers who interpret and apply laws

law a rule, usually made by a government, that is used to control the way in which people in a society behave

legislature people elected by citizens to work in government on their behalf. Elected representatives debate and vote on laws proposed by the executive branch.

manifesto a written statement of the beliefs, aims, and policies of an organization such as a political party

market the people who might want to buy something, or a part of the world where something is sold

media means of communication such as radio, television, newspapers, magazines, and the Internet, that reach or influence a large number of people

nomadic group of people who have no fixed home and move from place to place in search of food, water

petition a formal written request signed by many people

political party an organised group of people with similar political aims and ideas

politics the name for the way groups of people make decisions about running the country

polling station a building where people go to vote in an election

pollution the action or process of making land, water, air, etc., dirty and unsafe or unsuitable to use

priest person who has the power to carry out services and duties for their religion

propaganda ideas or information that are often false or exaggerated that are spread in order to influence public opinion in a particular way

public service a service provided by a government to help its people, such as a health service or fire service

regime a particular form or system, of government

regional government a government that only has control over a specific small area or region

representative democracy system of government in which citizens elect people to represent them to run the government and make decisions on their behalf

republic a state in which supreme power is held by the people and their elected representatives, and which has an elected or nominated president rather than a monarch

society the people of a country make up the society of that country

state a nation or territory under one government.

succession the way people inherit a title, such as monarch

tax a sum of money people have to pay their government so it can do its work and provide services they need or want

trade the action of buying and selling goods and services

welfare help given, especially by a government or state, to people who need it

FIND OUT MORE

Books

All About Politics (Big Questions), Dorling Kindersley, 2016

How to Build Your Own Country Valerie Wyatt, Wayland, 2017

The Politics Book, Paul Kelly, Dorling Kindersley, 2013

U.S. Government: What You Need to Know (Fact Files) Melissa Ferguson, Capstone Press, 2017

Websites

There is a helpful guide to how politics works and how it affects all of us at:
www.everyvotecounts.org.uk/how-politics-works/what-is-politics/

Find out more about how the UK government works at:
www.gov.uk/government/how-government-works

There is a brief guide to different systems of government at: http://news.bbc.co.uk/cbbcnews/hi/find_out/guides/world/united_nations/types_of_government/

There is a helpful table about the different kinds of democracy at:
www.democracy-building.info/systems-democracy.html

INDEX